Mother Goose Time

presents

Nursery Rhymes

pictures by chris lensch

First published by Experience Early Learning Company
7243 Scotchwood Lane, Grawn, Michigan 49637 USA

Text Copyright ©2014 by Experience Early Learning Co.
Printed and Bound in the USA

ISBN: 978-1-937954-11-6
visit us at **www.ExperienceEarlyLearning.com**

Mother Goose Time
presents

Nursery Rhymes

pictures by chris lensch

This Little Piggy

This little piggy went to market.

This little piggy stayed home.

1

This little piggy had roast beef. This little piggy had none.

And this little piggy cried "Wee, wee, wee!"
All the way home.

1, 2, Buckle My Shoe

1, 2, buckle my shoe.
3, 4, shut the door.
5, 6, pick up sticks.
7, 8, lay them straight.
9, 10, do it again.

1, 2
3, 4
5, 6
7, 8
9, 10

Hot Cross Buns

Hot cross buns,
Hot cross buns,
One a penny, two a penny,
Hot cross buns.
If your daughters don't like 'em,
Give 'em to your sons.
One a penny, two a penny,
Hot cross buns.

4

Itsy Bitsy Spider

The itsy bitsy spider,
Climbed up the waterspout.
Down came the rain,
And washed the spider out.
Out came the sun,
And dried up all the rain.
And the itsy bitsy spider,
Climbed up the spout again.

There Was a Crooked Man

There was a crooked man,
And he walked a crooked mile.
He found a crooked sixpence,
Against a crooked stile.
He bought a crooked cat,
Which caught a crooked mouse.
And they all lived together,
In a crooked little house.

6

Little Boy Blue

Little Boy Blue, come blow your horn.

The sheep's in the meadow, the cow's in the corn.

Where is the boy who looks after the sheep?

He's under the haystack, fast asleep!

Mary Had a Little Lamb

Mary had a little lamb,

Its fleece was white as snow.

Everywhere that Mary went,

The lamb was sure to go.

It followed her to school one day,

Which was against the rule.

It made the children laugh and play,

To see a lamb at school.

Old King Cole

Old King Cole was a merry old soul,

And a merry old soul was he;

He called for his wife,

And he called for his bowl,

And he called for his fiddlers three.

Little Miss Muffet

Little Miss Muffet,
Sat on a tuffet,
Eating her curds and whey.
Along came a spider,
And sat down beside her,
And frightened Miss Muffet away!

Twinkle, Twinkle, Little Star

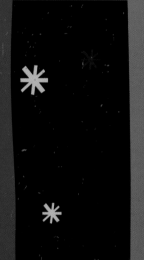

Twinkle, twinkle, little star,
How I wonder what you are.
Up above the world so high,
Like a diamond in the sky.
Twinkle, twinkle, little star,
How I wonder what you are.

There Was an Old Woman

There was an old woman,
Who lived in a shoe.
She had so many children,
She knew just what to do.
She gave them some broth,
And baked them some bread,
Then gave them hugs and kisses,
And sent them off to bed.

14

Sing a Song of Sixpence

Sing a song of sixpence,
A pocket full of rye;
Four and twenty blackbirds,
Baked in a pie.
When the pie was opened,
The birds began to sing;
Wasn't that a dainty dish,
To set before the king?

15

Little Jack Horner

Little Jack Horner,

Sat in a corner,

Eating a piece of pie.

He put in his thumb,

And pulled out a plum,

And said, "What a good boy am I!"

16

Humpty Dumpty

Humpty Dumpty sat on a wall,
Humpty Dumpty had a great fall.
All the king's horses,
And all the king's men,
Couldn't put Humpty together again!

17

Hickory, Dickory, Dock

Hickory, dickory, dock,
The mouse ran up the clock.
The clock struck one,
The mouse ran down,
Hickory, dickory, dock!

18

Pat-a-Cake

Pat-a-cake, pat-a-cake, baker's man.
Bake me a cake as fast as you can.
Roll it and pat it, then mark it with a "B",
Put it in the oven for my baby and me!

19

Baa, Baa, Black Sheep

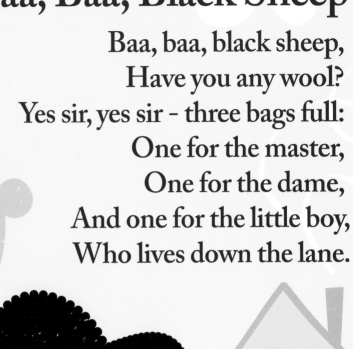

Baa, baa, black sheep,
Have you any wool?
Yes sir, yes sir - three bags full:
One for the master,
One for the dame,
And one for the little boy,
Who lives down the lane.

Hey Diddle Diddle

Hey diddle diddle,
The cat and the fiddle,

The cow jumped over the moon.

The little dog laughed,
To see such a sight,

And the dish ran away with the spoon.

experience™
Early Learning

Experience Early Learning specializes in the development and publishing of research-based curriculum, books, music and authentic assessment tools for early childhood teachers and parents around the world. Our mission is to inspire children to experience learning through creative expression, play and open-ended discovery. We believe educational materials that invite children to participate with their whole self (mind, body and spirit) support on-going development and encourage children to become the authors of their own unique learning stories.

www.ExperienceEarlyLearning.com